# The Romantic Tradition in American Literature

# The Romantic Tradition in American Literature

*Advisory Editor*

HAROLD BLOOM
Professor of English, Yale University

# POEMS

### BY EDWARD C. PINKNEY

## ARNO PRESS

**A NEW YORK TIMES COMPANY**

New York • 1972

Reprint Edition 1972 by Arno Press Inc.

The Romantic Tradition in American Literature
ISBN for complete set:  0-405-04620-0
See last pages of this volume for titles.

Manufactured in the United States of America

ഗദ൭ദ൭ദ൭ദ൭ദ൭ദ൭ദ

**Library of Congress Cataloging in Publication Data**

Pinkney, Edward Coote, 1802-1828.
   Poems.

   (The Romantic tradition in American literature)
   I.  Series.
PS2591.A1  1972          811'.2       72-4970
ISBN 0-405-04640-5

# POEMS.

# POEMS

## BY EDWARD C. PINKNEY.

Baltimore:

JOSEPH ROBINSON.

1838.

# CONTENTS.

---

# ITALY.

### I.

Know'st thou the land which lovers ought to choose?
Like blessings there descend the sparkling dews;
In gleaming streams the chrystal rivers run,
The purple vintage clusters in the sun;
Odours of flowers haunt the balmy breeze,
Rich fruits hang high upon the vernant trees;
And vivid blossoms gem the shady groves,
Where bright-plumed birds discourse their careless loves.
Beloved! — speed we from this sullen strand
Until thy light feet press that green shore's yellow sand.

### II.

Look seaward thence, and nought shall meet thine eye
But fairy isles like paintings on the sky;
And, flying fast and free before the gale,
The gaudy vessel with its glancing sail;
And waters glittering in the glare of noon,
Or touched with silver by the stars and moon,
Or flecked with broken lines of crimson light
When the far fisher's fire affronts the night.
Lovely as loved! towards that smiling shore
Bear we our household gods, to fix for evermore.

### III.

It looks a dimple on the face of earth,
The seal of beauty, and the shrine of mirth;
Nature is delicate and graceful there,
The place's genius, feminine and fair:
The winds are awed, nor dare to breathe aloud;
The air seems never to have borne a cloud,
Save where volcànoes send to heav'n their curled
And solemn smokes, like altars of the world.
Thrice beautiful! — to that delightful spot
Carry our married hearts, and be all pain forgot.

### IV.

There Art, too, shows, when Nature's beauty palls,
Her sculptured marbles, and her pictured walls;
And there are forms in which they both conspire
To whisper themes that know not how to tire:
The speaking ruins in that gentle clime
Have but been hallowed by the hand of Time,
And each can mutely prompt some thought of flame —
The meanest stone is not without a name.
Then come, beloved! — hasten o'er the sea
To build our happy hearth in blooming Italy.

# THE INDIAN'S BRIDE.

## I.

Why is that graceful female here
With yon red hunter of the deer?
Of gentle mien and shape, she seems
    For civil halls designed,
Yet with the stately savage walks
    As she were of his kind.
Look on her leafy diadem,
Enriched with many a floral gem:
Those simple ornaments about
Her candid brow, disclose
The loitering Spring's last violet,
And Summer's earliest rose;
But not a flower lies breathing there,
Sweet as herself, or half so fair.
Exchanging lustre with the sun,
    A part of day she strays —
A glancing, living, human smile,
    On nature's face she plays.
Can none instruct me what are these
Companions of the lofty trees? —

## II.

Intent to blend with his her lot,
Fate formed her all that he was not ;
And, as by mere unlikeness thoughts
    Associate we see,
Their hearts from very difference caugh
    A perfect sympathy.
The household gooddess here to be
Of that one dusky votary, —
She left her pallid countrymen,
    An earthling most divine,
And sought in this sequestered wood
    A solitary shrine.
Behold them roaming hand in hand,
Like night and sleep, along the land ;
Observe their movements : — he for her
    Restrains his active stride,
While she assumes a bolder gait
    To ramble at his side :
Thus, even as the steps they frame,
Their souls fast alter to the same.
The one forsakes ferocity,
    And momently grows mild ;
The other tempers more and more
    The artful with the wild.
She humanizes him, and he
Educates her to liberty.

## III.

Oh say not, they must soon be old,
Their limbs prove faint, their breasts feel cold !

Yet envy I that sylvan pair,
     More than my words express,
The singular beauty of their lot,
     And seeming happiness.
They have not been reduced to share
The painful pleasures of despair :
Their sun declines not in the sky,
     Nor are their wishes cast,
Like shadows of the afternoon,
     Repining towards the past :
With nought to dread, or to repent,
The present yields them full content.
In solitude there is no crime;
     Their actions are all free,
And passion lends their way of life
     The only dignity ;
And how should they have any cares? —
Whose interest contends with theirs? —

### IV.

The world, or all they know of it,
Is theirs : — for them the stars are lit;
For them the earth beneath is green,
     The heavens above are bright ;
For them the moon doth wax and wane,
     And decorate the night ;
For them the branches of those trees
Wave music in the vernal breeze ;
For them upon that dancing spray
     The free bird sits and sings,
And glit'ring insects flit about
     Upon delighted wings ;
     2*

For them that brook, the brakes among,
Murmurs its small and drowsy song;
For them the many coloured clouds
    Their shapes diversify,
And change at once, like smiles and frowns,
    Th' expression of the sky.
For them, and by them, all is gay,
And fresh and beautiful as they :
The images their minds receive,
    Their minds assimilate,
To outward forms imparting thus
    The glory of their state.
Could aught be painted otherwise
Than fair, seen through her star-bright eyes ?
He too, because she fills his sight,
    Each object falsely sees ;
The pleasure that he has in her,
    Makes all things seem to please.
And this is love; — and it is life
They lead, — that Indian and his wife.

# THE VOYAGER'S SONG.

---

" A tradition prevailed among the natives of Puerto Rico, that in the Isle of Bimini, one of the Lucayos, there was a fountain of such wonder-ful virtue as to renew the youth and recal the vigour of every person who bathed in its salutary waters. In hopes of finding this grand resto-rative, Ponce de Leon and his followers, ranged through the islands, searching with fruitless solicitude for the fountain, which was the chief object of the expedition."  *Robertson's America.*

---

### I.

Sound trumpets, ho ! — weigh anchor — loosen sail —
The seaward flying banners chide delay ;
As if 'twere heaven that breathes this kindly gale,
Our life-like bark beneath it speeds away.
Flit we, a gliding dream, with troublous motion,
Across the slumbers of uneasy ocean ;
And furl our canvass by a happier land,
So fraught with emanations from the sun,
That potable gold streams through the sand
Where element should run.

### II.

Onward, my friends, to that bright, florid isle,
The jewel of a smooth and silver sea,
With springs on which perennial summers smile
A power of causing immortality.

For Bimini;—in its enchanted ground,
The hallowed fountains we would seek, are found;
Bathed in the waters of those mystic wells,
The frame starts up in renovated truth,
And, freed from time's deforming spells,
Resumes its proper youth.

### III.

Hail, better birth! — once more my feelings all
A graven image to themselves shall make,
And, placed upon my heart for pedestal,
That glorious idol long will keep awake
Their natural religion, nor be cast
To earth by Age, the great Iconoclast.
As from Gadara's founts they once could come,
Charm-called, from these Love's genii shall arise,
And build their perdurable home,
Miranda, in thine eyes.

### IV.

By Nature wisely gifted, not destroyed
With golden presents, like the Roman maid, —
A sublunary paradise enjoyed,
Shall teach thee bliss incapable of shade; —
And Eden ours, nor angry gods, nor men,
Nor star-clad Fates, can take from us again.
Superiour to animal decay,
Sun of that perfect heaven, thou'lt calmly see
Stag, raven, phenix, drop away
With *human* transiency.

### V.

Thus rich in being, — beautiful, — adored,
Fear not exhausting pleasure's precious mine ;
The wondrous waters we approach, when poured
On passion's lees, supply the wasted wine :
Then be thy bosom's tenant prodigal,
And confident of termless carnival.
Like idle yellow leaves afloat on time,
Let others lapse to death's pacific sea, —
We'll fade nor fall, but sport sublime
In green eternity.

### VI.

The envious years, which steal our pleasures, thou
May'st call at once, like magic memory, back,
And, as they pass o'er thine unwithering brow,
Efface their footsteps ere they form a track.
Thy bloom with wilful weeping never stain,
Perpetual life must not belong to pain.
For me, — this world has not yet been a place
Conscious of joys so great as will be mine,
Because the light has kissed no face
Forever fair as thine.

## SONG.

We break the glass, whose sacred wine
　　To some beloved health we drain,
Lest future pledges, less divine,
　　Should e'er the hallowed toy profane;
And thus I broke a heart, that poured
　　Its tide of feelings out for thee,
In draughts, by after-times deplored,
　　Yet dear to memory.

But still the old empassioned ways
　　And habits of my mind remain,
And still unhappy light displays
　　Thine image chambered in my brain,
And still it looks as when the hours
　　Went by like flights of singing birds,
Or that soft chain of spoken flowers,
　　And airy gems, thy words.

## A PICTURE SONG.

How may this little tablet feign the features of a face,
Which o'er-informs with loveliness its proper share of
    space ;
Or human hands on ivory enable us to see
The charms, that all must wonder at, thou work of Gods,
    in thee !

But yet, methinks, that sunny smile familiar stories tells,
And I should know these placid eyes, two shaded chrystal
    wells ;
Nor can my soul, the limner's art attesting with a sigh,
Forget the blood, that decked thy cheek, as rosy clouds
    the sky.

They could not semble what thou art, more excellent than
    fair,
As soft as sleep or pity is, and pure as mountain-air;
But here are common, earthly hues, to such an aspect
    wrought,
That none, save thine, can seem so like the beautiful of
    thought.

The song I sing, thy likeness like, is painful mimicry
Of something better, which is now a memory to me,

Who have upon life's frozen sea arrived the icy spot,
Where men's magnetic feelings show their guiding task
    forgot.

The sportive hopes, that used to chase their shifting sha-
    dows on,
Like children playing in the sun, are gone — forever gone;
And on a careless, sullen peace, my double-fronted mind,
Like Janus when his gates were shut, looks forward and
    behind.

Apollo placed his harp, of old, awhile upon a stone,
Which has resounded since, when struck, a breaking
    harp-string's tone ;
And thus my heart, though wholly now from early soft-
    ness free,
If touchèd, will yield the music yet, it first received of
    thee.

# LINES

FROM THE PORT FOLIO OF H········.

### I.

WE met upon the world's wide face,
 When each of us was young —
We parted soon, and to her place
 A darker spirit sprung;
A feeling such as must have stirred
The Roman's bosom when he heard,
 Beneath the trembling ground,
The God, his genius, marching forth
From the old city of his mirth,
 To lively music's sound.

A sense it was, that I could see
 The angel leave my side —
That thenceforth my prosperity
 Must be a falling tide;
A strange and omnious belief,
That in spring-time the yellow leaf
 Had fallen on my hours;
And that all hope must be most vain,
Of finding on my path again,
 Its former, vanished flowers.

3

But thou, the idol of my few
   And fleeting better days —
The light that cheered when life was new
   My being with its rays —
And though, alas! — its joy be gone,
Art yet, like tomb-lamps, shining on
   The phantoms of my mind —
The memories of many a dream
Floating on thought's fantastic stream,
   Like storm-clouds on the wind!

Is thy life but the wayward child
   Of fever in the heart,
In part a crowd of fancies wild,
   Of ill-made efforts part?
Are such accurst familiars thine,
As by thee were made early mine?
   And is it as with me —
Doth hope in birthless ashes lie,
And seems the sun an hostile eye
   Thy pains well-pleased to see?

I trust, not so : — though thou hast been
   An evil star to mine,
Let all of good the world has seen
   Hang ever upon thine.
May thy suns those of summer be,
And time show as one joy to thee,
   Like thine own nature pure :
Thou didst but rouse, within my breast,
The sleeping devils from a rest,
   That could not long endure.

The firstlings of my simple song
  Were offered to thy name :
Again the altar, idle long,
  In worship rears its flame.
My sacrifice of sullen years,
My many hecatombs of tears,
  No happier hours recall —
Yet may thy wandering thoughts restore
To one who ever loved thee more
  Than fickle fortune's all.

And now, farewell ! — and although here
  Men hate the source of pain,
I hold these and thy follies dear,
  Nor of thy faults complain.
For my misused and blighted powers,
My waste of miserable hours,
  I will accuse thee not : —
The fool who could from self depart,
And take for fate one human heart,
  Deserved no better lot.

I reck of mine the less, because
  In wiser moods I feel
A doubtful question of its cause,
  And nature, on me steal —
An ancient notion, that time flings
Our pains and pleasures from his wings
  With much equality —
And that, in reason, happiness
Both of accession and decrease
  Incapable must be.

# LINES

*FROM THE PORT FOLIO OF H----------*

## II.

By woods and groves the oracles
  Of the old age were nursed ;
To Brutus came in solitude
  The spectral warning first,
When murdered Cesar's mighty shade
The sanguine homicide dismayed,
  And fantasy rehearsed
The ides of March, and, not in vain,
Showed forth Philippi's penal plain.

In loneliness I heard my hopes
  Prononnce, " Let us depart !"
And saw my mind — a Marius —
  Desponding o'er my heart :
The evil genius, long concealed,
To thought's keen eye itself revealed,
  Unfolding like a chart,
But rolled away, and left me free
As Stoicks once aspired to be.

It brought, thou spirit of my breast,
　And Naiad of the tears,
Which have been welling coldly there,
　Although unshed, for years!
It brought in kindness or in hate,
The final menaces of fate,
　But prompted no base fears —
Ah, could I with ill feelings see
Aught, love, so near allied to thee?

The drowsy harbinger of death,
　That slumber dull and deep,
Is welcome, and I would not wake
　Till thou dost join my sleep.
Life's conscious calm, — the flapping sail, —
The stagnant sea nor tide nor gale
　In pleasing motion keep, —
Oppress me ; and I wish release
From this to more substantial peace.

Star of that sea ! — the cynosure
　Of magnet-passions, long !
A ceaseless apparition, and
　A very ocular song ! —
My skies have changed their hemisphere,
And forfeited thy radiant cheer :
　Thy shadow still is strong ;
And beaming darkness, follows me,
Far duskier than obscurity.

Star of that sea ! — its currents bear
　My vessel to the bourne,

3*

Whence neither busy voyager
　Nor pilgrim may return.
Such consummation I can brook,
Yet with a fixed and lingering look,
　Must anxiously discern
The far horizon, where thy rays
Surceased to light my night-like days.

Unwise, or most unfortunate,
　My way was; let the sign,
The proof of it, be simply this —
　Thou art not, wert not, mine!
For 'tis the wont of chance to bless
Pursuit, if patient, with success;
　And envy may repine,
That, commonly, some triumph must
Be won by every lasting lust.

How I have lived imports not now
　I am about to die,
Else I might chide thee that my life
　Has been a stifled sigh:
Yes, life; for times beyond the line
Our parting traced, appear not mine,
　Or of a world gone by;
And often almost would evince,
My soul had transmigrated since.

Pass wasted powers; alike the grave,
　To which I fast go down,
Will give the joy of nothingness
　To me and to renown:

Unto its careless tenants, fame
Is idle as that gilded name,
    Of vanity the crown,
Helvetian hands inscribe upon
The forehead of a skeleton.

List the last cadence of a lay,
    That, closing as begun,
Is governed by a note of pain,
    Oh, lost and worshipped one! —
None shall attend a sadder strain,
Till Memnon's statue stand again
    To mourn the setting sun, —
Nor sweeter, if my numbers seem
To share the nature of their theme.

## TO * * * * * *

'Twas eve; the broadly shining sun
Its long, celestial course, had run;
The twilight heaven, so soft and blue,
Met earth in tender interview,
Ev'n as the angel met of yore
His gifted mortal paramour,
Woman, a child of morning then, —
A spirit still, — compared with men.
Like happy islands of the sky,
The gleaming clouds reposed on high,
Each fixed sublime, deprived of motion,
A Delos to the airy ocean.
Upon the stirless shore no breeze
Shook the green drapery of the trees,
Or, rebel to tranquillity,
Awoke a ripple on the sea.
Nor, in a more tumultuous sound,
Were the world's audible breathings drowned;
The low strange hum of herbage growing,
The vice of hidden waters flowing,
Made songs of nature, which the ear
Could scarcely be pronounced to hear;
But noise had furled its subtile wings,
And moved not through material things,
All which lay calm as they had been
Parts of the painter's mimic scene.

'Twas eve; my thoughts belong to thee,
Thou shape of separate memory!
When, like a stream to lands of flame,
Unto my mind a vision came.
Methought, from human haunts and strife
Remote, we lived a loving life;
Our wedded spirits seemed to blend
In harmony too sweet to end,
Such concord as the echoes cherish
Fondly, but leave at length to perish.
Wet rain-stars are thy lucid eyes,
The Hyades of earthly skies,
But then upon my heart they shone,
As shines on snow the fervid sun.
And fast went by those moments bright,
Like meteors shooting through the night;
But faster fleeted the wild dream,
That clothed them with their transient beam.
Yet love can years to days condense,
And long appeared that life intense;
It was, — to give a better measure
Than time, — a century of pleasure.

# ELYSIUM.

(*FROM AN UNFINISHED POEM.*)

SHE dwelleth in Elysium ; there,
Like Echo floating in the air ;
Feeding on light as feed the flowers,
She fleets away uncounted hours,
Where halcyon Peace, among, the blest,
Sits brooding o'er her tranquil nest.

She needs no impulse ; one she is,
Whom thought supplies with ample bliss :
The fancies fashioned in her mind
By heaven, are after its own kind ;
Like sky-reflections in a lake,
Whose calm no winds occur to break.

Her memory is purified,
And she seems never to have sighed :
She hath forgot the way to weep,
Her being is a joyous sleep ;
The mere imagining of pain,
Hath passed, and cannot come again.

Except of pleasure most intense
And constant, she hath lost all sense ;

Her life is day without a night,
An endless, innocent delight;
No chance her happiness now mars,
Howe'er Fate twine *her* wreaths of stars

And palpable and pure, the part,
Which pleasure playeth with her heart;
For every joy that seeks the maid,
Foregoes its common painful shade,
Like shapes that issue from the grove,
Arcadian, dedicate to Jove.

# EVERGREENS.

### *To * * * * * *.*

WHEN Summer's sunny hues adorn
  Sky, forest, hill and meadow,
The foliage of the evergreens,
  In contrast, seems a shadow

But when the tints of autumn have
  Their sober reign asserted,
The landscape that cold shadow shows,
  Into a light converted.

Thus thoughts that frown upon our mirth
  Will smile upon our sorrow,
And many dark fears of to-day
  May be bright hopes to-morrow.

And thine unfading image thus
  Shall often cheer my sadness,
Though now its constant looks reprove
  A momentary gladness.

# SERENADE

Look out upon the stars, my love,
And shame them with thine eyes,
On which, than on the lights above,
There hang more destinies.
Night's beauty is the harmony
Of blending shades and light;
Then, Lady, up, — look out, and be
A sister to the night! —

Sleep not! — thine image wakes for aye,
Within my watching breast:
Sleep not! — from her soft sleep should fly,
Who robs all hearts of rest.
Nay, Lady, from thy slumbers break,
And make this darkness gay,
With looks, whose brightness well might make
Of darker nights a day.

## SONG.

I NEED not name thy thrilling name,
   Though now I drink to thee, my dear,
Since all sounds shape that magic word,
   That fall upon my ear, — Mary;
And silence, with a wakeful voice,
   Speaks it in accents loudly free,
As darkness hath a light that shows
   Thy gentle face to me, — Mary.

I pledge thee in the grape's pure soul,
   With scarce one hope, and many fears,
Mixt, were I of a melting mood,
   With many bitter tears, — Mary —
I pledge thee, and the empty cup
   Emblems this hollow life of mine,
To which, a gone enchantment, thou
   No more wilt be the wine, — Mary,

# A HEALTH.

I FILL this cup to one made up of loveliness alone,
A woman, of her gentle sex the seeming paragon;
To whom the better elements and kindly stars have given,
A form so fair, that, like the air, 'tis less of earth than
    heaven.

Her every tone is music's own, like those of morning
    birds,
And something more than melody dwells ever in her
    words;
The coinage of her heart are they, and from her lips each
    flows
As one may see the burthened bee forth issue from the
    rose.

Affections are as thoughts to her, the measures of her
    hours;
Her feelings have the fragrancy, the freshness, of young
    flowers;
And lovely passions, changing oft, so fill her, she appears
The image of themselves by turns, — the idol of past
    years!

Of her bright face one glance will trace a picture on the
    brain,
And of her voice in echoing hearts a sound must long re-
    main,

But memory such as mine of her so very much endears,
When death is nigh my latest sigh will not be life's but
    hers.

I filled this cup to one made up of loveliness alone,
A woman, of her gentle sex the seeming paragon —
Her health! and would on earth there stood some more of
    such a frame,
That life might be all poetry, and weariness a name.

# PROLOGUE.

*DELIVERED AT THE GREEK BENEFIT, IN BALTIMORE---1832.*

" ILLE, NON EGO."

### I.

As one, who long upon his couch hath lain
Subdued by sickness to a slave of pain,
When time and sudden health his strength repair,
Springs jocund to his feet, and walks the air ;
So Greece, through centuries a prostrate land,
At length starts up — forever may she stand —

### II.

Since smiling Liberty, the sun thrice blest,
That had its rising in our happy west,
Extends its radiance, eastward, to that shore,
The place of Gods whom yet our hearts adore ;
And, hailed by loud acclaim of thousands, hath
Been worshipped with a more than Magian faith,
With slain Barbarian hosts for sacrifice,
And burning fleets for holocausts of price :

4*

Shall we, who almost placed it in the sky,
Fail to assist the magnanimity,
With which, regardless of much pressing want,
They greet their fair and heavenly visitant?
Forbid it, Justice! we detest the state,
Which, knowing that mortality must rate
By mere comparison things dark or bright, —
Would make its fame as painters form a light,
By circumjacent blackness—we are free,
And so could wish the total earth to be.
Greece *shall*,—Greece *is*,—each old, heroic shade,
Draws, with her living sons, his spectral blade,
And combats, proud of times so like his own,
Like Theseus' ghost at storied Marathon.

### III.

"The Last of Grecians," — is become a phrase,
Improper in these new triumphant days :
The swords well wielded against Turkish bands,
Are not unworthy of those mighty hands,
Which overthrew the haughty Persian, when
Pausanias and Leonidas were men.

### IV.

To-night, the useful and the pleasing claim,
Still more than commonly, to seem the same ;
For, pleasing you, we aid, " in our degree,"
A struggling nation's strife for liberty, —
The strife whose voice from this great world demands,
What mine of you beseeches — " clap your hands !"

## SONG.

DAY departs this upper air,
  My lively, lovely lady;
And the eve-star sparkles fair,
  And our good steeds are ready.
Leave, leave these loveless halls,
  So lordly though they be; —
Come, come — affection calls —
  Away at once with me!

Sweet thy words in sense as sound,
  And gladly do I hear them;
Though thy kinsmen are around,
  And tamer bosoms fear them.
Mount, mount, — I'll keep thee, dear,
  In safety as we ride; —
On, on — my heart is here,
  My sword is at my side!

# THE WIDOW'S SONG.

I BURN no incense, hang no wreath,
  On this, thine early tomb :
Such cannot cheer the place of death,
  But only mock its gloom.
Here odorous smoke and breathing flower
  No grateful influence shed ;
They lose their perfume and their power,
  When offered to the dead.

And if, as is the Afghaun's creed,
  The spirit may return,
A disembodied sense to feed,
  On fragrance, near its urn —
It is enough, that she, whom thou
  Did'st love in living years,
Sits desolate beside it now,
  And falls these heavy tears.

## TO * * * * * *

With Wordsworth's, " She was a phantom of delight," &c.

Accept this portraiture of thee,
　　Revealed to Wordsworth in a dream —
One less immortal stays with me,
　　Whose airy hues thine own may seem :
Mental reflection of thy light,
A rainbow beautiful and bright ;
　　A shining lamp of constant ray,
To which my fancy shall be slave ;
　　A shaping that cannot decay,
Until it moulder in my grave.—
The image-breaker, Time, may mar
　　All meaner sculpture of my mind,
But in its darkness, like a star,
　　Thy semblance shall remain enshrined :
Nor would I that the sullen thing
　　Its place in being should resign,
While, like a casket rich with gems,
　　It treasures forms so fair as thine.

## SONG.

THOSE starry eyes, those starry eyes,
　　Those eyes that used to be
Unto my heart, as beacon-lights
　　To pilgrims of the sea ! —

I see them yet, I see them yet,
　　Though long since quenched and gone —
I could not live enlumined by
　　The common sun alone.

Could they seem thus, could they seem thus,
　　If but a memory ? —
Ah, yes ! upon this wintry earth,
　　They burn no more for me.

## ON PARTING.

Alas ! our pleasant moments fly
  On rapid wings away,
While those recorded with a sigh,
  Mock us by long delay.

Time, — envious time, — loves not to be
  In company with mirth,
But makes malignant pause to see
  The work of pain on earth.

# RODOLPH,

## A FRAGMENT.

" Call these forms from under ground,
With a soft and happy sound."

*Fletcher.*

" There is an order
Of mortals on the earth, who do become
Old in their youth, and die ere middle age,
Without the violence of warlike death ;
Some perishing of pleasure—some of study—
Some worn with toil—some of mere weariness,
Some of disease—and some insanity—
And some of withered, or of broken hearts ;
For this last is a malady which slays
More than are numbered in the lists of fate,
Taking all shapes, and bearing many names.

*Lord Byron.*

# DEDICATION.

Sweet Promiser! — If now to thee
(No halcyon on the wintry sea
    Of troubled feeling yet)
I dedicate this idle rhyme,
Woven to cheer the laggard time,
    Though wisdom would forget;
Learn that when as a funeral train
The mournful moments crossed my brain,
I could not but remember hours,
Which wore bright coronals of flowers,
And came successively to me,
Like notes of heart-felt melody.
Learn further, that with these was shown
A phantom fairer far — thine own —
An apparition none can know,
Or guess of, saving only *thou*.
As for this story of an age
That saw life fanciful as dreams,
Thy gem-like eye will scan its page;
And if, with sounds of sleepy streams,
Thy voice make music of my lays —
Could they obtain a dearer praise?

# RODOLPH.

## PART I.

### I.

THE Summer's heir on land and sea
Had thrown his parting glance,
And Winter taken angrily
His waste inheritance.
The winds in stormy revelry
Sported beneath a frowning sky;
The chafing waves with hollow roar
Tumbled upon the shaken shore,
And sent their spray in upward shower
To Rodolph's proud ancestral towers,
Whose station from its mural crown
A regal look cast sternly down.

### II.

At such a season, his domain
The lord at last arrived again,
Changed to the sight, and scarce the same
Grown old in heart, infirm of frame.
His earlier years had been too blest
For anguish not to curse the rest :

5*

Men, like the Dioscuri, dwell
Alternately in heaven and hell.
Let those, whose lives are in their prime,
Use to the uttermost the time;
For as with the enchanted thrall
Of Eblis and his fatal hall,
When a short period departs,
The flame shall kindle in their hearts.
Thou only, mighty Love! — canst will
Much herald good, much after-ill;
Thou holdest human hearts in fee,
And art the Second Destiny.
He loved — he won — and whom? — he sighed
First *for*, next *with*, another's bride:
To both extremes of feeling, — strong
Or feeble, — the same signs belong,
And sighs may the expression be
Of ecstasy or agony.

\*    \*    \*    \*    \*    \*    \*    \*    \*    \*

### III.

Like rarest porcelain were they,
Moulded of accidental clay:
She, loving, lovely, kind, and fair —
He, wise, and fortunate, and brave —
You'll easily suppose they were
A passionate and radiant pair,
Lighting the scenes else dark and cold,
As the sepulchral lamps of old,
A subterranean cave.
'Tis pity that their loves were vices,
And purchased at such painful prices;

'Tis pity, and Delight deplores,
That grief allays her golden stores.
Yet if all chance brought rapture here,
Life would become a ceaseless fear
To leave a world, then rightly dear.
Two kindred mysteries* — are bright,
And cloud-like, in the southern sky ;
A shadow and its sister-light,
Around the pole they float on high,
Linked in a strong though sightless chain,
The types of pleasure and of pain.

## IV.

There was an age, they tell us, when
Eros and Anteros dwelt with men,
Ere selfishness had backward driven
The wrathful deities to heaven ;
Then gods forsook their outshone skies,
For stars mistaking female eyes ;
Woman was true, and man though free
Was faithful in idolatry.
No dial needed they to measure
Unsighing being — Time was Pleasure ;
And lustres, never dimmed by tears,
Were not misnamed from lustrous years.
Alas ! that such a tale must seem
The fiction of a dreaming dream ! —
Is it but fable ? — has that age
Shone only on the poet's page,

* The Magellan clouds.

Where earth, a luminous sphere portrayed,
Revolves not both in sun and shade?—
No!—happy love, too seldom known,
May make it for awhile our own.

### V.

Yes, although fleeting rapidly,
It sometimes may be ours,
And he was gladsome as the bee*
Which always sleeps in flowers.
Might this endure?—her husband came
At an untimely tide,
But ere his tongue pronounced her shame,
Slain suddenly, he died.
'Twas whispered by whose hand he fell,
And Rodolph's prosperous loves were gone.
The lady sought a convent-cell,
And lived in penitence alone;
Thrice blest, that she the waves among
Of ebbing pleasure staid not long,
To watch the sullen tide, and find
The hideous shapings left behind.
Such, sinking to its slimy bed,
Old Nile upon the antique land,
Where Time's inviolate temples stand
Hath ne'er deposited.
Happy, the monster of that Nile,
The vast and vigorous crocodile;
Happy, because his dying-day
Is unpreceded by decay:

* The Florisomnis.                † The Pyramids.

We perish slowly — loss of breath
Only completes one piece-meal death.

## VI.

She ceased to smile back on the sun,
Their task the Destinies had done;
And earth, which gave, resumed the charms;
Whose freshness withered in its arms;
But never walked upon its face,
Nor mouldered in its dull embrace,
A creature fitter to prepare
Sorrow, or social joy to share:
When her the latter-life required,
A vital harmony expired;
And in that melancholy hour,
Nature displayed its saddest power,
Subtracting from man's darkened eye
Beauties that seemed unmeant to die,
And claiming deeper sympathy
Than even when the wise or brave
Descend into an early grave.
We grieve when morning puts to flight
The pleasant visions of the night;
And surely we shall have good leave,
When a fair woman dies, to grieve.
Whither have fled that shape, and gleam
Of thought — the woman, and the dream? —
Whither have fled that inner light,
And benefactress of our sight? —
Nothing in answer aught can show,
Only thus much of each we know —

The dream may visit us again,
She left for aye the sons of men ! —
Death may in part discharge its debt,
Half render back its trust —
Life may redeem her likeness yet,
Reanimate her dust ;
But both will bear another name,
Nor, like the dream, appear the same.

## VII.

While Hope attends her sacred fire,
All joy rejoices in its pyre :
Once quenched, what ray the flame renews?
What but calamity ensues ?
When ill-report disgraced his name,
And turned to infamy his fame,
Bearing from home his blighted prime,
He journeyed to some distant clime,
Where babbling rumour could not trace
His footsteps to a resting place.
Mean while, the quest of happiness
He made, dispairing of success ;
Unhoped, but not pursued the less,
It urged around the world its flight
Away from him, like day from night.
There are, who deem of misery
As if it ever craved to die :
They err ; the full of soul regard,
More than the calm, their graves with hate ;
The loss of such a life is hard,
And, ending their eventful fate,

From so much into nothing must
The change be pain — from *this* to dust ! —
To fill the chasms of the breast,
'Tis happiness they seek, not rest ;
Wishing for something to amend
Existence, they must shun its end ;
And this the princely will betrays
To many sufferings and days.

## VIII.

As sunk, avoiding mortal touch,
The Cabalist's discovered treasure,
So met his sight, escaped his clutch,
Many appearances of pleasure,
Deceitful as that airy lie,
The child of vapour and the sky.*
Which cheats the thirsty Arab's eye,
Only the palm, heat-loving tree,
Or bird of happy Araby,
May burn, and not to die :
Philosophy has lost the power†
From ashes to reform a flower;
Magic and Alchemy no more
Men's primal strength and youth restore,
Nor could those great and dream-like arts,
While flourishing, revoke their hearts :
The feelings rise regenerate never,
But, once consumed, are gone forever.
*  *  *  *  *  *  *
*  *  *  *  *  *  *

* The Mirage.                    † Palingenesy.

# RODOLPH.

## PART II.

### I.

How feels the guiltless dreamer, who
With idly curious gaze
Has let his mind's glance wander through
The relics of past days ?—
As feels the pilgrim that has scanned,
Within their skirting wall,
The moon-lit marbles of some grand
Disburied capital;
Masses of whiteness and of gloom,
The darkly bright remains
Of desolate palace, empty tomb,
And desecrated fanes : —
For in the ruins of old hours,
Remembrance haply sees
Temples, and tombs, and palaces,
Not different from these.

### II.

But such mere musings could not now
Move Rodolph's lip, or curl his brow :

His countenance had lost its free
And former fine transparency,
Nor would, as once, his spirit pass
Its fleshly mask, like light through glass.
In his sad aspect seemed to be
Troubled reflections of a life,
Nourished by passion, spent in strife—
Gleams, as of drowned antiquity
From cities underneath the sea
Which glooms in famous Galilee.

### III.

In the calm scene he viewed was aught,
That might disturb a froward thought?
He saw, new-married to the air,
The tranquil, waveless deep,
Reposing in a night as fair
As woman's softest sleep :
Peaceful and silent, were met all
The elements in festival,
And the wide universe seemed to be
One clear obscure transparency.
Could such a quiet Fancy wake?
And doth she from her slumbers break,
As drowsy mortals often will,
When lamps go out, or clocks fall still?
No less than when the Wind-God's breath
Blackens the wilderness beneath,
Until contrasted stars blaze bright
With their own proper heavenly light,

And almost make the gazer sigh,
For our unseen mythology.
Motion or rest, a sound, a glance,
Alike rouse memory from its trance.

### IV.

Perhaps, presentiment of ill
Might shake him — hearts are prophets still —
What though the fount of Castaly
Not now stains leaves with prophecy? —
What though are of another age
Omens, and Sibyl's boding page? —
Augurs and oracles resign
Their voices — fear can still divine:
Dreams and hand-writings on the wall
Need not foretell our fortune's fall;
Domitian in his galleries,*
The soul all hostile advents sees,
As in the mirror-stone;
Like shadows by a brilliant day
Cast down from falcons on their prey;
Or watery demons, in strong light,
By haunted waves of fountains old,
Shown indistinctly to the sight
Of the inquisitive and bold.
The mind is capable to show
Thoughts of so dim a feature,
That consciousness can only know
Their presence, not their nature;

* Vide Suetonius.

Things, which, like fleeting insect-mothers,
Supply recording life to others,
And forthwith lose their own.

## V.

He backed his steed, and took his way
Where a large cemetery lay,
Beaming beneath the star-light gay,
A white spot in the greenery,
Semblant of what it well might be —
A blossom unto which the earth
As a spring-favour yielded birth.
They looked for his return in vain,
Homeward he never rode again.
What boots it to protract the verse,
In which his story I rehearse? —
He had won safely through the past,
The growing sickness smote at last:
His vassals found him on the morn,
Senseless beside his lady's urn ;
And they beheld with wonderment
His visage — like a bow unbent,
From the distorting mind unstrung,
By painful thought no longer wrung,
It offered once more to their gaze
The cheerful mien of former days,
And on it the fixt smile had place,
Which lights the Memnon's marble face.

## VI.

Hot fever raged in Rodolph's brain,
Till tortured reason fled,
And madness a delirious reign
Asserted in its stead;
And then he raved of many crimes,
Achieved in shadows of all climes;
Of Indian islands, tropic seas,
Ships winged before the flying breeze;
Of peace, of war, of wine, of blood,
Of love and hate, of changing mood
Or changing scenery;
And often on his language hung
The accents of an alien tongue,
But still they circled one dark deed,
As charmed men that magic weed,
The herb of Normandy.*
He spoke of one too dearly loved,
And one unwisely slain,
Of an affection hardly proved
By murder done in vain —
Affection which no time could tire,
Constant as emeralds in fire,
Like that which weds insanity
To the sole truth that earth may see.
Some fragments of his speech my rhyme
Shall rescue from the grasp of time,
As trophies, by the march of song,
In tuneless triumph borne along.

*" L'Herbe Maudite.

6*

## VII.

" The evil hour in which you traced
" Your name upon my heart, is passed,
" And hidden fires or lightning-flashes
" Have since reduced it into ashes ;
" Yet oft will busy thought unrol
" That fragile, scorched, and blackened scroll,
" And shrink to find the spell, your name,
" A legend uneffaced by flame.

## VIII.

" Who spoke that lawless, sounding word,
" So early hushed, so long unheard ? —
" Its syllables came o'er my brain,
" Like the last trumpet's call ;
" And, starting from their graves again,
" My buried thoughts, in fear and pain,
" Are gathering one and all.
" The pictured memories hid by grief
" Come forth in beautiful relief,
" Freed from their former thrall —
" As, through the torch-touched rust of years
" A waxen painting re-appears
" On a sepulchral wall.

## VIII.

" Thy face revives the face of one,
" That *lived* in other days —

" Whose fading phantom had begun
" To fail my fancy's gaze ;
" Though shadowed forth too long and well,
" As my sad history may tell.
" Thy face revives the face of one,
" That *loved* in other days —
" Of whom or thought or speech was none,
" Less passionate than praise :
" So much she beautified the place
" Replete with her in time and space.
" Thy face revives the face of one,
" That *died* in other days —
" Who bought, not borrowed, from the sun
" Its scarcely needed rays ;
" And thousand charms could not concur
" To make thee fair, — yet unlike her.
" It is herself ! — the gods in pity
" Restore her from the silent city ! —
" Now, where are they, that falsely said,
" Her form in stirless dust was laid ?
" Who reared the lying pyramid,
" Whose epitaph, and lamp, and flame,
" Told that her heavenward home lay hid
" In its sky-pointing frame ?
" She is not dead — behold her eye,
" That portion of a summer-sky :
" She is not dead — her cheeks are rife
" With rosy clouds of blooming life :
" She is not dead — the shining hair
" Is wreathed about her forehead fair,
" As when I saw in better hours
" Her gentle shape of living mirth,

" And trod with her upon all flowers
" Worn by the festive earth.
" Time interposed — it was not Death,
" He could not stop her spicy breath —
" But hearts and hands have met once more ;
" We will be happy as before ;
" And my crime-sullied memory
" Like a re-written code* shall be,
" Full of the poetry of truth,
" The annals of a second youth,
" Illuminations blazoned bright
" With sun-born tints of golden-light.

IX.

" If, memory, on thy silent shore,
" The stream of time hath left
" Some broken hopes, plans quick no more,
" And thoughts of breath bereft ;
" The strong belief in happiness,
" It could but half destroy ;
" The now-dead generous carelessness,
" That hung around the boy ;
" And feelings which the subtile wave
" Bore not through later years —
" Such wrecks the smiles of wisdom crave
" Not less than passion's tears. —
" But thou, the sweetest of Eve's daughters,
" Genius† of that shore, and those waters ! —
" A music visible, a light
" Like lamps unto an infant's sight ! —

* " Codex Rescriptus."　　　　　† " Genius Loci."

" A temple of celestial soul,
" Too lovely for aught ill to mar,
" Which Love from Beauty's planet stole,
" The morn and evening star ! —
" Come thou, and pass away with me
" From haunts unworthy of thy smile,
" And find in some far, sunny sea,
" A lonely, laughing isle,
" Where we may through all pleasures rove,
" And live like votaries of love,
" Drinking the sparkling stream of years,
" Pure, and unmixt with worm-wood tears.
\*    \*    \*    \*    \*    \*    \*

### X.

" Why have I, speaking thus to thee,
" Vague sense that these things may not be ? —
" Strange flitting fires each other chase,
" Like meteors, through a cheerless space :
" My sight grows heavy, and my breast
" By something mountainous is prest;
" And, in my veins, the lazy blood
" Is not that eager, rushing flood,
" It was when thou wert nigh,
" Nor will my limbs avail to bear
" My feeble, sickly body, where
" Thou standest moveless by.
" I feel a weary wish to close
" Mine eye-lids in a long repose;
" But fear that thou wilt fly,
" And let me wake alone to sigh
" That one so beautiful *could* die !

## XI.

" Author of my unhappiness ! —
" Let me thy lip and small hand press.
" Since love increases when the day
" Its object's presence makes is done,
" And takes from night a warmer ray,
" As did the Fountain of the Sun,*
" Thine, so long absent, should forgive
" The death of one I slew for thee —
" Resentment cannot bid him live,
" Pardon perchance may me.
" Obdurate Lady, even thine eye
" To my fond prayer makes no reply ;
" And hast thou come then from afar,
" A coldly re-appearing star ? —
" Thou never lov'dst : — thy constancy
" Would answer else aright to mine :
" In one so lovely, love must be
" Preserved still fresh, like grapes in wine.
" Thy smiles were but a shining mask,
" Thy vows no more than vocal air,
" If thou canst let me vainly ask
" Relief from this despair.
" By all that I have borne and bear,
" She fades to unsubstantial air !–

\*    \*    \*    \*    \*    \*    \*

## XII.

" The perturbation of my soul
" Subsides as I approach the goal ;

* ᵛ Fons Solis."

" Yet dreamt I one was here but now,
" Whose brow was like her ivory brow.
" When shall we two meet again,
" And not, as last, to part in pain? —
" Spring shall leave to rear the flowers,
" And Autumn to let fall the showers;
" Summer shall forbear to glow,
" And Winter doff its veil of snow;
" Man shall know no more to mourn,
" The age of miracles return:
" Woman shall forget to range,
" And fortune and the moon to change;
" Tears and tides shall cease to flow,
" The sea and life their storms forego;
" Opportunity shall stay
" The wings on which it flies away;
" Memory the past shall scan,
" Yet see not, like a drowning man,
" Fast upon the bitter wave
" The ship depart, that ought to save;
" Noon and midnight shall have met,
" The stars have risen where they set;
" Ere, though but in sleep, we twain
" Can dream one hope to meet again. —
" She lies amid the sluggish mould,
" Her ardent heart has long been cold!
" Above it wave the idle weeds,
" On it the sordid earth-worm feeds.
" Mine too is buried there — her knell
" Served also for its passing bell:
" It died — and would have known 't was time,
" Without that melancholy chime.

" That knell ! — I feel its strokes again,
" Like stunning blows upon my brain ;
" I listen yet the dissonant laughter
" Of the same bell, some moments after ;
" And now the frequent ding-dong hear,
" With which it mimics hope and fear

## XIII.

" Ay, wrapt around a whiter breast,
" The shroud her body doth invest ;
" But in that other world, her grave,
" My soul and body both inter,
" There to enjoy the rest they crave,
" And, if at all, arise with her :
" Never may either wake, unless
" To her, and former happiness ! —
" Yet how am I assured that rest
" Will ever bless the aching breast,
" Which passion has so long possessed ?—
" At baffled death's oblivious art
" This love perchance will mock,
" Deep-dwelling in my festering heart,
" A reptile in its rock :
" The warm and tender violet
" Beside the glaciers grows,
" Although with frosty airs beset,
" And everlasting snows ;
" So, lying in obstruction chill,
" This stronger flower may flourish still.
" Oh, in the earth, ye furies, let
" My thoughtful clay all thought forget :

" Suffer no sparkles of hot pain
" Among mine ashes to remain :
" Give, give me utterly to prove
" Insentient of the pangs of love ! —
" — Why waver thus these forms ? — there lies
" A palpable blackness on mine eyes ;
" And yet the figures gleam
" With the impressive energy,
" Which clothes the phantoms that we see
" Shown by a fever-dream.
" How the air thickens — all things move —
" 'Tis night — 'tis chaos — my lost love ! —"

## XIV.

He perished.   None wept o'er his bier,
Although above such things we weep,
And rest obtains the useless tear,
Due rather to the state of sleep ; —
For why ? — because the common faith
Of passion is averse from death ;
Yet Jove, the sages all declare,
Granted the Argive mother's* prayer.

* Cydippe.  See Herod.

7

# THE OLD TREE.

(From the Note-Book of a Traveller.)

## I.

AND is it gone, that venerable tree,
The old spectator of my infancy! —
It used to stand upon this very spot,
And now almost its absence is forgot.
I knew its mighty strength had known decay,
Its heart, like every old one, shrunk away,
But dreamt not that its frame would fall, ere mine
At all partook my weary soul's decline.

## II.

The great reformist, that each day removes
The old, yet never on the old improves,
The dotard, Time, that like a child destroys,
As sport or spleen may prompt, his ancient toys,
And shapes their ruins into something new —
Has planted other playthings where it grew.

The wind pursues an unobstructed course,
Which once among its leaves delayed perforce;
The harmless Hamadryad, that, of yore,
Inhabited its bole, subsists no more;
Its roots have long since felt the ruthless plow —
There is no vestige of its glories now!
But in my mind, which doth not soon forget,
That venerable tree is growing yet;
Nourished, like those wild plants that feed on air,
By thoughts of years unconversant with care,
And visions such as pass ere man grows wholly
A fiendish thing, or mischief adds to folly.
I still behold it with my fancy's eye,
A vernant record of the days gone by:
I see not the sweet form and face more plain,
Whose memory *was* a weight upon my brain.
— Dear to my song, and dearer to my soul,
Who knew but half my heart, yet had the whole
Sun of my life, whose presence and whose flight
Its brief day caused, and never ending night!
Must this delightless verse, which is indeed
The mere wild product of a worthless weed,
(But which, like sun-flowers, turns a loving face
Towards the lost light, and scorns its birth and place,)
End with such cold allusion unto you,
To whom, in youth, my very dreams were true?
It must; I have no more of that soft kind,
* My age is not the same, nor is my mind.

* Horace.


FINIS.

# The Romantic Tradition in American Literature

An Arno Press Collection

Alcott, A. Bronson, editor. **Conversations with Children on the Gospels.** Boston, 1836/1837. Two volumes in one.

Bartol, C[yrus] A. **Discourses on the Christian Spirit and Life.** 2nd edition. Boston, 1850.

Boker, George H[enry]. **Poems of the War.** Boston, 1864.

Brooks, Charles T. **Poems, Original and Translated.** Selected and edited by W. P. Andrews. Boston, 1885.

Brownell, Henry Howard. **War-Lyrics** and Other Poems. Boston, 1866.

Brownson, O[restes] A. **Essays and Reviews Chiefly on Theology, Politics, and Socialism.** New York, 1852.

Channing, [William] Ellery (The Younger). **Poems.** Boston, 1843.

Channing, [William] Ellery (The Younger). **Poems of Sixty-Five Years.** Edited by F. B. Sanborn. Philadelphia and Concord, 1902.

Chivers, Thomas Holley. **Eonchs of Ruby:** A Gift of Love. New York, 1851.

Chivers, Thomas Holley. **Virginalia;** or, Songs of My Summer Nights. (Reprinted from *Research Classics*, No. 2, 1942). Philadelphia, 1853.

Cooke, Philip Pendleton. **Froissart Ballads,** and Other Poems. Philadelphia, 1847.

Cranch, Christopher Pearse. **The Bird and the Bell,** with Other Poems. Boston, 1875.

[Dall], Caroline W. Healey, editor. **Margaret and Her Friends.** Boston, 1895.

[D'Arusmont], Frances Wright. **A Few Days in Athens.** Boston, 1850.

Everett, Edward. **Orations and Speeches,** on Various Occasions. Boston, 1836.

Holland, J[osiah] G[ilbert]. **The Marble Prophecy,** and Other Poems. New York, 1872.

Huntington, William Reed. **Sonnets and a Dream.** Jamaica, N. Y., 1899.

Jackson, Helen [Hunt]. **Poems.** Boston, 1892.

Miller, Joaquin (Cincinnatus Hiner Miller). **The Complete Poetical Works of Joaquin Miller.** San Francisco, 1897.

Parker, Theodore. **A Discourse of Matters Pertaining to Religion.** Boston, 1842.

Pinkney, Edward C. **Poems.** Baltimore, 1838.

Reed, Sampson. **Observations on the Growth of the Mind.** *Including,* **Genius** (Reprinted from *Aesthetic Papers,* Boston, 1849). 5th edition. Boston, 1859.

Sill, Edward Rowland. **The Poetical Works of Edward Rowland Sill.** Boston and New York, 1906.

Simms, William Gilmore. **Poems:** Descriptive, Dramatic, Legendary and Contemplative. New York, 1853. Two volumes in one.

Simms, William Gilmore, editor. **War Poetry of the South.** New York, 1866.

Stickney, Trumbull. **The Poems of Trumbull Stickney.** Boston and New York, 1905.

Timrod, Henry. **The Poems of Henry Timrod.** Edited by Paul H. Hayne. New York, 1873.

Trowbridge, John Townsend. **The Poetical Works of John Townsend Trowbridge.** Boston and New York, 1903.

Very, Jones. **Essays and Poems.** [Edited by R. W. Emerson]. Boston, 1839.

Very, Jones. **Poems and Essays.** Boston and New York, 1886.

White, Richard Grant, editor. **Poetry:** Lyrical, Narrative, and Satirical of the Civil War. New York, 1866.

Wilde, Richard Henry. **Hesperia:** A Poem. Edited by His Son (William Wilde). Boston, 1867.

Willis, Nathaniel Parker. **The Poems, Sacred, Passionate, and Humorous, of Nathaniel Parker Willis.** New York, 1868.